Eileen Dunlop

Scottish Homes
through the ages

illustrated by John Harrold

Richard Drew Publishing, Glasgow

✳◇✳◇✳◇✳◇✳◇✳◇✳◇✳◇✳◇✳◇✳◇✳◇✳◇✳◇✳◇✳◇✳◇✳

British Library Cataloguing in Publication Data
Dunlop, Eileen
Scottish homes through the ages.
1. Dwellings — Scotland — Juvenile literature
2. Architecture, Domestic — Scotland — Juvenile literature
I. Title   II. Kamm, Antony
728'.09411   NA7334
ISBN 0-86267-087-X
ISBN 0-86267-086-1 Pbk

First Published 1985 by Richard Drew Publishing Ltd,
6 Clairmont Gardens, Glasgow G3 7LW

Copyright © 1985 Eileen Dunlop and Antony Kamm

Designed by James W Murray
Printed and bound in Great Britain
Set in Raleigh by John Swain Ltd, Glasgow

F 5000 Years Ago

At one time, Scotland was completely covered by ice. When the ice finally melted and went away, dense forests grew. Now deer, boars and wild cattle roamed where before there had been just reindeer. As far as we know, the first people came to Scotland from the south, probably in boats, in about 7000 BC, or almost nine thousand years ago. They were hunters and fishermen. They lived in caves, and used stone tools to make spear-heads and fish-hooks out of antlers and bones. When they had to move away to better hunting grounds, they built themselves temporary homes of branches and skins.

As time went on, people learned how to grow crops and keep cattle, sheep and pigs. They needed permanent homes, which they built of large stones. Five thousand years ago there was a village at Skara Brae, on the shore of the island of Orkney. It consisted of a close cluster of one-roomed houses, joined by narrow covered passages. Each house had a door, seats, beds, cupboards and shelves, all made of stone. There was a hearth in the middle of the floor for the peat fire. The roofs were made of whalebone or bits of wood, covered over with turf. The inhabitants of Skara Brae had grain, which they grew. They ate meat from their own herds, from animals and sea-birds that they hunted, and from whales that they found stranded on the shore. They also caught fish and collected shellfish from the rocks.

Though the houses had drains which ran under the floors and out into the sea, they must have been terribly smelly to live in. They had no windows, and the rubbish and the bones of the animals and fish that had been eaten were heaped all over the roofs of the houses, just leaving holes for the smoke from the fires to escape.

In about 2500 BC a terrific storm covered the village with sand. The inhabitants fled. The houses remained buried until AD 1850, when another storm blew some of the sand away, revealing underneath the remains of the houses, as they can still be seen today.

2000 Years Ago

The inhabitants of Skara Brae were Stone Age people. In about 2000 BC, a new skill was brought to Scotland. Men learned how to melt down copper and tin together to make bronze. From the bronze, they made axe-heads, swords, ornaments and farming implements. Later, about 600 BC, they discovered how to make tools and weapons out of iron, which is a much tougher metal than bronze.

As more people came from Europe to settle in Scotland, the population grew. Good farming land became valuable. To protect themselves and their homes from raiders, farmers, especially in the north of Scotland, built hill-top villages of round stone huts with pointed thatched roofs. The village was fortified by a thick stone wall with stakes on top of it, and a deep ditch all round.

The first castles were great round towering structures known as brochs. Brochs were first built in about 100 BC and they continued in use for about six hundred years. They were mainly for defence against raiders who came from over the sea. Their remains are found only in Scotland.

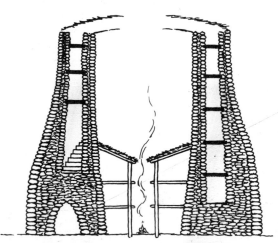

Brochs were made of rough stone blocks, fitted to each other without any mortar to bind them together. The only opening on the outside was a single heavy door. The centre of the broch was probably open to the sky. All the rooms were inside the thick double wall, and were reached by narrow, winding staircases.

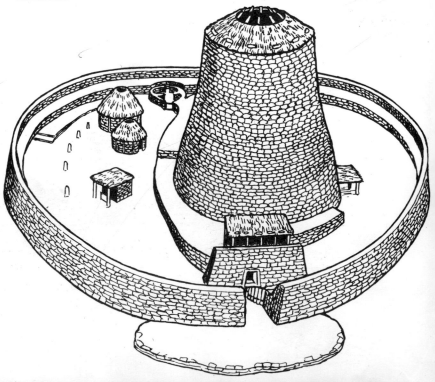

To protect themselves against robbers, and wolves as well, people who lived on lochs built themselves crannogs in the water itself. A crannog was a house of wood and thatch on an artificial island. It was joined to the shore by a narrow causeway hidden under the surface of the water. People went on living in crannogs until about AD 1450.

In the first and second centuries AD, many people lived in earth-houses, or weems. A weem was a stone hut, or a series of huts joined together, from which ran a stone-lined underground tunnel. Some of these tunnels were 60 metres long and had drains running under the floor-stones. While the tunnels were certainly used for storing grain and other provisions, there is evidence that people actually ate and slept in them too, perhaps in time of danger or cold weather.

Defensive walls were often laced with timber and branches to make them more difficult to knock down. When the wood was set on fire, either accidentally or on purpose, the heat melted the stones and fused them together. Walls in which this has happened are called 'vitrified' walls.

storage tank for shellfish

drain

1800 Years Ago

A typical dun had walls 5 metres thick, enclosing a space 20 metres across.

In western and southern Scotland are remains of low round forts, called duns. They may have been built as defences against invaders from the south. Duns had hollow walls like brochs, but they were only two storeys high. They continued to be built and lived in for a thousand years.

In AD 80, the invasion happened. The Romans came with their legions of soldiers, marching along their straight stone roads, determined to complete their occupation of Britain by conquering Scotland too. Wherever they went they built forts for their troops to live in.

Roman forts were built to a standard pattern and were surrounded by a high wooden wall and several deep ditches. Inside were rows of barracks for the men, and workshops, granaries, store-houses, bathhouses, a hospital, an administrative block and a centrally-heated house for the commander.

A camp commander's house was usually built round a courtyard, with rooms leading off it. The heating system, called a hypocaust, warmed the walls as well as the floor.

The Romans were great builders. To keep the northern tribes from attacking the lands they had conquered in the south, they built Hadrian's Wall right across north Britain. Then they built the Antonine Wall across Scotland from the Clyde to the Forth. Made of turf, with a wooden rampart on top, the Antonine Wall had 16 forts spaced out along the 60 kilometres of its length.

Twice, in AD 155 and 184, the northern Scottish tribes did manage to break through the Antonine Wall. Then, only about a hundred years after they had come to Scotland, the Romans packed up their belongings, destroyed their forts, and retreated to the other side of Hadrian's Wall. They left the land inhabited by four different peoples — in the north, the Picts; in the west, the Scots; in the south-west, the Britons; and in the south-east, the Angles.

A Roman bath-house was like a modern sauna. There was a changing-room, and cold, warm, hot and very hot rooms.

1300 Years Ago

When the Romans left Scotland, they took with them their knowledge of building. For about six hundred years most people went on living in the same kinds of homes as their ancestors had done. In places where there were few stones, they built huts from wooden poles interwoven with twigs and branches and then covered with clay — this method of building is called 'wattle and daub'. Bigger huts had screens in them to give some kind of privacy. The hearth was in the centre of the earth floor: the smoke from the fire escaped through the roof.

The first Christian missionaries came to Scotland from the south in about AD 400. In 563, the Irish monk Columba landed on the island of Iona with twelve companions. There they founded their first monastery and built a church, a guest-house, dining-hall, farm-houses and huts for the monks, all of timber and wattle and daub. Columba had two buildings for himself. One had a floor of planks of wood and served as his study and the monastery's library: in the other he slept on the bare ground with a stone for his pillow!

Columba and his followers established other monasteries in lonely coastal places and on islands where the monks could have quiet and seclusion. The buildings were now of stone. The monks lived in little round individual huts like beehives.

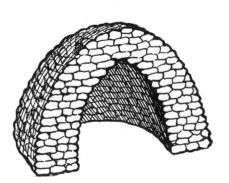

Some huts were made with double walls, separated at the bottom by a few layers of stones. The space between them was packed with grass and heather to make an insulated barrier against the cold.

The monks' beehive huts were corbelled; that is, the stones of the upper walls gradually overlapped the ones below until they met at the top, thus forming the roof.

The room at the far end had a roof and floor of stone. It was probably where food was stored.

In the north, Pictish people continued to build quite ingenious oval or round stone houses with several rooms. Some had two entrances closed by wooden doors. Roofs were corbelled or of timber, and covered with squares of turf on which the grass was allowed to continue to grow. The grass bound the turfs together, making the house warm and the roof fairly watertight. However, it also meant that when the outside doors were shut, there was nowhere for the smoke from the fire to get out. Perhaps people felt it was cosier that way!

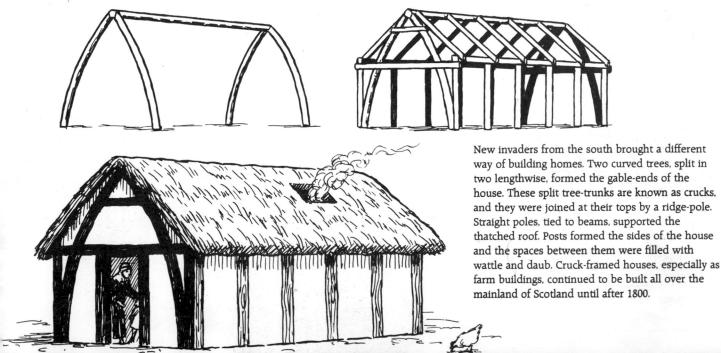

New invaders from the south brought a different way of building homes. Two curved trees, split in two lengthwise, formed the gable-ends of the house. These split tree-trunks are known as crucks, and they were joined at their tops by a ridge-pole. Straight poles, tied to beams, supported the thatched roof. Posts formed the sides of the house and the spaces between them were filled with wattle and daub. Cruck-framed houses, especially as farm buildings, continued to be built all over the mainland of Scotland until after 1800.

800 Years Ago

The Normans invaded England from France in 1066. However, there were other Normans who were later invited to come to Scotland by David I (1124–1153) and be his lords. They built 'motte and bailey' castles of timber and wattle and daub. Some of these castles had three storeys and contained a hall, living-room, bedrooms, servants' quarters, a sick-room and a chapel. The entrance could only be reached by a ladder, and there was a clever defensive system of ditches, log walls and bridges. The enclosure below the castle contained extra buildings for eating and sleeping, stables, store-houses and space for people who lived nearby to shelter with their flocks in time of danger.

'Motte' is from the same word as moat: it also means the mound of earth dug out of the ground to make the moat. A bailey is an area enclosed by a wall or fence.

The first towns began as 'burghs', small groups of houses built near a castle on each side of a single street. The burgh was a centre for trade and where craftsmen — clothmakers, tailors, leather-workers, shoemakers, metal-workers, butchers and bakers could work and offer their services. The gable-ends of the houses faced the street, on which the rubbish piled up — it was removed once a week, on Sundays. Some merchants and craftsmen had houses of two storeys with an outside staircase: the bottom floor was the shop. For everyone, just one room served as bedroom, sitting-room, dining-room and kitchen. There were no chairs, only stools or benches to sit on. A trestle-table was put up at mealtimes.

Country people worked as farmers. They did not own their land. It belonged to a landlord, to whom they paid rent in food or other produce or by doing extra work for him. Several families would live together in a settlement called a 'farm toun'. Their houses were low, triangular structures of wood, stones and thatch, without any windows. Cooking was done in a cauldron which hung over the fire from the roof. They slept on wooden beds or on straw mattresses on the floor and shared their smoky, smelly homes with their cattle and hens.

Farm toun homes like this were called 'cuppled houses'. Cupples are two beams tied together at their tops in the form of an upside-down V.

From about AD 800, Scotland suffered raids from the Norsemen, or Vikings as they came to be called: 'viking' in Old English meant 'pirate'. They came also to Shetland and Orkney and the north mainland to live as farmers and fishermen. Remains of some of their homes have been found at Jarlshof in Shetland, near an old Bronze Age and an Iron Age settlement. This house was originally about 20 metres long and had a roof of timber and turf. It had two rooms, a kitchen and a living-room with a hearth in the middle. The inhabitants slept on stone benches along the walls. Outside was a small bath-house. Two hundred years later, the house was enlarged. A byre was attached to the end of the living-room, with a stone-paved path leading right through it into the house.

700 Years Ago

Queen Margaret, wife of Malcolm III, founded a large Benedictine monastery at Dunfermline in about 1074. Her sons Edgar, Alexander I and David I, and some of their barons, also invited groups of monks to come from England and France to build monasteries in Scotland.

The chief purpose of a monastery was regularly to hold services of worship and to offer prayers to God. However, most monks (or canons or friars, as some of them were called) also helped the sick, the poor and those who were travelling; they spread learning by teaching and by making copies of books, and sometimes worked at farming.

There were a number of different Orders of monks. Each Order followed a different set of rules and had a slightly different way of life. At one time, there were more than forty monasteries in Scotland. The Cistercians built 11 monasteries in lonely places. The Augustinians (or Black Canons — they wore black cloaks), who had seven houses, went out more among the people and also preached in local churches. The tiny Order of Carthusians had just one monastery, at Perth, where its monks devoted their time to meditation and prayer, hardly ever speaking to each other.

Some Scottish monasteries were sacked by Henry VIII's English troops in 1545. Others were destroyed by mobs or were taken over by local lords or by the Crown. By 1600 all had ceased to exist as homes for men of the religious Orders.

The picture on the opposite page is of a monastery as it might have been in about 1250. There was a staircase from the dormitory right down into the church, so that no time would be wasted getting to services. There were eight services each day, three of them before dawn. Apart from the kitchen, there were only two fires in the whole place: one in a room for the canons called 'the warming-house', and the other in the novices' day-room, where those training to be canons were taught. The canons had only one or two meals a day, in the dining-room. Before meals, they washed their hands in a trough of running water set into the wall of the cloister. The cloister was a covered walk-way, where the canons could sit or walk and meditate. In the middle was a kitchen garden, where vegetables and herbs were grown.

dormitory

hospital

latrine block

novices' day-room

cloister

kitchen

600 Years Ago

Castles had no bathrooms, but they did have lavatories of a kind. These were usually in cubicles called garderobes, off a room or at the end of a passage. The waste went through a pipe sticking out of the castle wall or dropped down a chute into the moat, if there was one, or into a cess-pit. Another kind of garderobe projected out of the castle wall, as in the picture.

The great stone castles were built for defence and also for the comfort of the owner and his family, who had a set of rooms in a tower. There was no accommodation for the many servants. They just slept on the floor of the hall or in the kitchen.

At mealtimes, trestle-tables were set up in the hall and covered with cloths. The lord sat in a chair on the middle of the 'hie burde', or high table, which was usually on a raised dais at one end of the room. Minstrels used to play from a gallery at the other end. The lord's family and important guests sat on cushions on benches at either side of him. Other members of the household sat along the sides of the hall with their backs to the wall. Everyone wore a hat or head-dress at meals, to prevent headlice falling into the food. There were no forks. People ate with their fingers.

Cooking was done on a vast open fire. Kitchens got so hot that cooks often wore only loin-cloths and it was common for kitchen maids to die of heat. Most castles had a well. However, the main use of water was for cooking, especially of meat and fish which had been preserved in salt. People usually drank ale or wine. Nobody washed very much.

retainer's hall

lord's bedroom

lord's living-room

garderobe

guest rooms

lord's dining-hall

kitchen

well

Doune Castle, Perthshire, as it probably was soon after it was built in about 1390.

500 Years Ago

People of less importance than the nobles who owned castles still needed to protect themselves against attack, especially in the Borders. There were frequent skirmishes with the English, and between rival bands of cattle rustlers, or 'reivers', as they were called. Richer Borderers lived in plain towers with very few windows and just one entrance. The living quarters were on the upper floors, which could only be reached up a narrow circular-stairway, set clockwise so that an attacker could not easily use his sword.

At this time larger and more elaborate tower-houses were being built all over Scotland. They were popular because they were easy to defend and because they gave their owners some chance of comfort and privacy: the servants, of course, had neither — they still slept where they could on the floors. However, even the richest people had little furniture — a chair for the lord of the house, benches and stools, beds for the more important members of the household, some chests in which to store clothes, candlesticks, plates of pewter or silver, mugs and a few spoons: the knives used at table were the ones that men carried around with them. Trestle-tables were set up for meals, and basins were provided for people to wash their hands in after eating. Otherwise there might be just one table, its top marked off with squares as an aid to counting. Very little else was needed. The

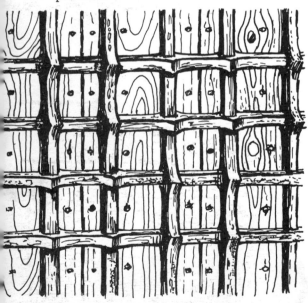

Most Border towers had only one room on each floor. If the tower was within a wooden or stone enclosure (called a 'peel') it was known as a peel-tower.

Entrances were usually defended by a heavy barred door of two thicknesses of planks and inside that a yett — a grill of strong interlocking iron bars. These yetts were so effective that in 1606 the Privy Council passed an order that the yetts in all strongholds in the Borders should be destroyed, except those in the homes of trustworthy barons.

men spent most of their time out of doors. The women could sit on cushions at stone window seats. Floors were covered with rushes, which were only occasionally changed. The walls were hung with tapestries.

Rooms had no doors to them. Glass was beginning to be used in windows. Often only the top part of a window had glass in it, to let in light. The bottom part was fitted with shutters, or 'shots', which could be opened to let in air from outside. A window with shutters was called a shot-window.

The hall was on the first floor, to be farther away from the main entrance in case of an attack. To make it more difficult for an attacker to reach the private rooms above, you usually had to cross the length of the hall to get to the staircase to the upper storeys. All the time you were crossing the floor of the hall, you could be watched through a spy-hole in the wall from a room built inside the wall. For the walls were massively thick. One tower-house had a spy-hole built through the back of the fire-place in the hall.

In Glasgow and Edinburgh, rich merchants and craftsmen were pulling down their old wooden houses and building themselves homes of stone, with wooden floors and thatched roofs. There might be a bedroom for the owner of the house. Otherwise, everyone still lived and slept in one room on the first floor, reached by a stairway in a courtyard at the back of the house. There was little furniture. Apart from a bed, which would have been a four-poster with curtains round it to keep out draughts, one Edinburgh house in 1530 contained only a counting table, a cupboard, a chair and a bench. The ground floor of such a house was the shop, which opened out on to the street.

The most uncomfortable place in a castle or tower-house was the pit, or prison. Often a pit could only be reached through a hatch in the ceiling. It had no windows. The only light came through a ventilation shaft.

Houses in the towns had no drains. Waste and rubbish of all kinds were just thrown into the street and left to stink. As a result, there were frequent attacks of plague.

400 Years Ago

At Flodden in 1513, James IV and most of his army were slaughtered by the English. Though the battle was fought fifty miles away from Edinburgh, it had a profound effect on the homes of people who lived there afterwards. The Town Council ordered a defensive wall to be built around three sides of the city — the fourth was protected by the Nor' Loch, where Princes Street Gardens now are. Though the wall was not finished for 47 years, it meant that for a long time all new houses were built inside it, in an area not much more than half-a-mile square. As the population grew, the only way to build was upwards. Edinburgh became a mass of towering tenement blocks, set on each side of alleys so narrow that often you could lean out of the window and shake hands with a neighbour across the street.

All kinds of people lived in one tenement block — merchants, noblemen, craftsmen, lawyers, labourers, beggars. The poorer families occupied the floors at the bottom and at the very top of the building. There were no lavatories and no bathrooms — in any case most people did not take off their underwear during the winter for fear of catching cold. Rubbish and slops were tipped out of the windows into the streets, in which pigs rooted during the day.

Farm workers lived in smelly squalor, too. Their homes were low hovels without windows. They were cruck-framed, with roofs of straw or heather thatch, and walls of turf or rough stones, with the spaces in between filled in with clay. Everyone lived, ate and slept in the one room, which they shared with cows, sheep and chickens. There might be a chair for the head of the household. Others sat on stools or rough benches or crouched on the earth floor. Cooking was done in an iron cauldron, which dangled from the roof over the fire.

Living in a burgh was probably just as smelly — there was a street in Culross which was, and still is, called Stinking Wynd. However, stone houses with thatched roofs were being built at the end of the 16th century. The walls were covered with harling, a mixture of plaster and small stones which was then left to dry. This gave protection against the weather. Harling is still used today on the walls of houses in Scotland.

The living-quarters in these houses were on the first floor. Steps led up to them from the street. Things were now being done, too, to

Claypotts Castle, built between 1569 and 1588, has two towers at opposite ends of the connecting building, making a Z-shape. Other houses were built in the shape of an L, an H or an E.

improve existing houses. In 1594, the Scottish Parliament passed an Act ordering the provost of every burgh to examine each house and to require its occupants to make any necessary repairs 'within a year and a day'.

Now that there was less need for heavily-fortified castles, tower-houses were becomong more elaborate, and more comfortable. Often they had more than one tower. There was still very little furniture, for it was expensive and had to be imported from abroad, mainly from Flanders. However, coverings for walls, tables and beds were rich and colourful. At mealtimes, table-cloths were of 'English green', a material like the covering of a modern snooker table. Tapestries on the walls had intricate patterns, or depicted religious or legendary scenes, hunting, battles or people at work on the land or in the vineyards.

The big house at Culross, known as the 'Palace', was built in stages between 1597 and 1611. James VI is said to have stayed there in 1617, and in some of the rooms you can still see the panelled walls and ceilings decorated as they were at the time with pictures and patterns. Some of the roofs of richer homes were now being made of curved red clay tiles, called pantiles. Originally these pantiles were made in Holland. Sailors who went across from the port of Culross to deliver coal and salt, brought them back as ballast to keep their little ships steady on the return journey.

300 Years Ago

Up to the end of the 17th century, most houses in Glasgow, except manses and the homes of the richer people, were built of wood, with thatched roofs. Streets were littered with dungheaps, peat-stacks and sometimes haystacks too. In the Trongate there was such a stream of sewage flowing down the street that people had to build stepping-stones to get into and out of their houses. In 1652 nearly a third of Glasgow was burned to the ground. The city magistrates, hearing that Edinburgh had a fire-engine, sent someone to examine it. As a result, they made one for themselves. It cannot have been a very successful machine. In 1667 another fire destroyed over six hundred homes. It was after this that the magistrates ordered that all new homes in Glasgow should be built entirely of stone.

Great changes took place in rich homes during the 17th century. The family now had their own dining-room, with a table set in the middle of the floor and chairs all round it. Table manners were better, too, and people were beginning to use forks for eating, instead of their fingers: though until after 1750, if you were going to a wedding feast or a public dinner, you had to take your own knife and fork in case none were provided. In many families, a clean linen or damask table-cloth was provided every day, and napkins for people to wipe their hands and mouths with. China plates, cups, saucers and bowls were coming into fashion. People were very proud of their china, because it was so difficult to transport over the rough roads without breaking.

There was a separate 'with-drawing room' — we now call it just a drawing-room —, where the family retired to relax after meals. It had comfortable padded chairs and small tables, sometimes with coloured marble tops. There might be a few rugs on the polished wooden floor. Windows were much larger now and were made entirely of panes of glass. Thick curtains helped to keep out the cold at night. As furniture was often moved from house to house — many Scottish nobles had a home also in London —, cupboards and chests were often fitted with iron handles so that they could more easily be carried.

Bedrooms were often used also as places in which to receive guests. So as well as the bed and chests for clothes, there might be easy chairs and tables. The bed was made up with blankets and sheets — or rather, one sheet, which was folded over at the bottom in a special Scottish way, so that the top and sides were open but the foot was closed.

Servants had a separate room in which to eat, though some of them slept in the same rooms as their masters and mistresses. Their beds were folded up and pushed under the big bed during the daytime. There was much work for servants to do. When the maids had finished the housework and their tasks in the kitchen, the laundry or the dairy, they might be kept at spinning until 9 p.m.

People in these times seem to have been keener on cleaning their homes and washing clothes and bed-linen and table-cloths than on keeping themselves clean. The fine new homes that were now being

Especially in the towns, big houses were being built that had their main rooms on the ground floor. Argyll's Lodging in Stirling, built in about 1630, with its courtyard and its towers, still looks like a castle, but it had a lot of rooms, including a ballroom and two kitchens.

Crofters' cottages were often built of dry stones (without mortar) and a roof of thatch weighted down with rocks. The windows were just small holes without glass. There was only one room, in the centre of which was the hearth. Cottages like these were still being lived in at the beginning of the 20th century.

built in Glasgow and some other towns had a separate room in which people could wash, in water brought in from a pump outside. In the country, most of the big houses had no such room, though there might be a cottage to which men could go to have a plunge in a tub of cold water!

In the Lowlands, important people in a village, like the leading farmers, the brewer and the miller, might have houses of two storeys with several rooms. People of slightly less importance — merchants, officials of the coal mine, the tailor, the shoe-maker — had smaller homes. A house with two rooms was known as a 'but and ben'. The but was kitchen and living-room, and where the grown-up daughters and female servants slept. The head of the household, with his wife and young children, slept in the ben. Grown-up sons slept in an attic made by laying planks across the beams which supported the roof.

Other villagers, including the schoolmaster, lived in one-room homes, measuring only about 6 by 4½ metres. Here, the whole family ate and slept and made many of the things they needed — cheese, cloth, candles, beer, leather. In some areas, anyone who had their own pigs had to keep them indoors too. The poorer people paid rent to a landlord, either in food or by doing work for him.

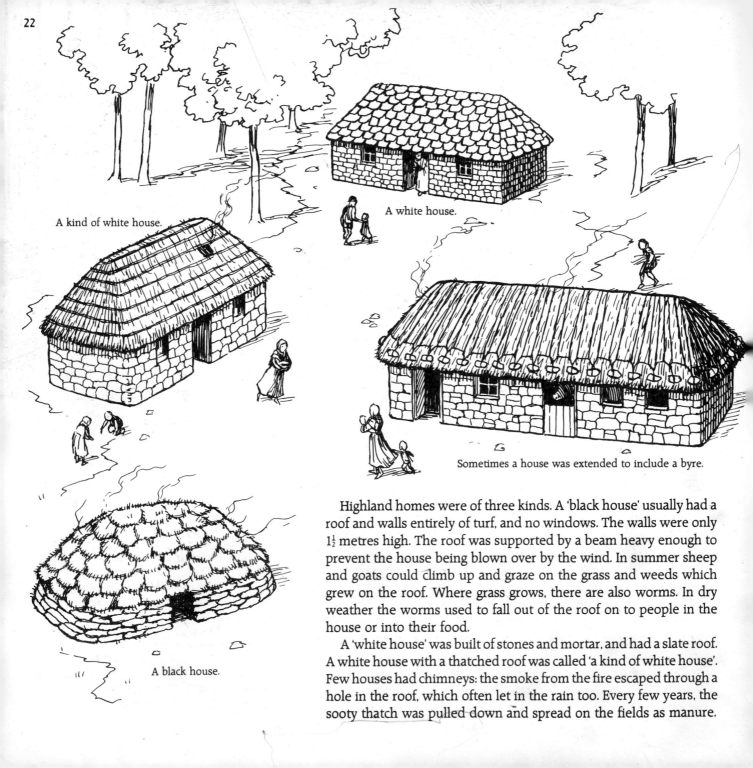

A kind of white house.

A white house.

Sometimes a house was extended to include a byre.

A black house.

Highland homes were of three kinds. A 'black house' usually had a roof and walls entirely of turf, and no windows. The walls were only 1½ metres high. The roof was supported by a beam heavy enough to prevent the house being blown over by the wind. In summer sheep and goats could climb up and graze on the grass and weeds which grew on the roof. Where grass grows, there are also worms. In dry weather the worms used to fall out of the roof on to people in the house or into their food.

A 'white house' was built of stones and mortar, and had a slate roof. A white house with a thatched roof was called 'a kind of white house'. Few houses had chimneys: the smoke from the fire escaped through a hole in the roof, which often let in the rain too. Every few years, the sooty thatch was pulled down and spread on the fields as manure.

Highland homes had hardly any furniture. There might be just one drinking mug — when there was a party, it was handed round from guest to guest. Otherwise, people drank from shallow wooden bowls, and ate from wooden platters. The men carried their knives, and sometimes their forks too, around with them. When they had cut up their own meat, they handed their knife and fork to the women, and ate with their fingers.

There was no need for any kind of lavatory. People just went out to the nearest bit of boggy ground. However, what with farm animals in the home, and dungheaps piling up outside the front door, Highland houses were still very dirty and smelly. A laird once ordered people on his estate to remove their dungheaps. One old lady reckoned she had cheated him: she got a spade and shovelled her dungheap inside her house!

A Highland chief's house might be 30 metres long and divided by partitions into several rooms, of which one at the end was occupied by cows. The roof was supported on wooden beams. The windows had glass in them, but no curtains. At night the rooms were lit by candles, which the women made out of suet from the carcases of sheep and cows. The floor was earth, stamped flat. For furniture there would be just a table, a few benches and stools and some chests — and a shelf of books. The wooden beds were made in the form of boxes with sliding panels down the side which could be closed during the day. However, Highlanders often preferred to sleep on a mattress of heather or straw on the floor, or in the open air on the bare ground, covered with their plaids.

200 Years Ago

At least, in Highland homes, there was usually a stream nearby from which water could be got for drinking, cooking and washing. After about 1760, some Scottish towns had pipes made of lead which brought water from the nearest river to wells in the streets. Perth had a row of small wells on each side of its main streets, to which people came to collect their water. Some Glasgow houses even had their own piped water supply. Water had been piped to wells in Edinburgh since 1681. Special water-carriers — the men in red jackets and the women in thick coats and black hats — spent all their time carrying it on their backs in heavy wooden casks up the narrow stairs of the tenement blocks, some of which were 15 storeys high.

Conditions in Edinburgh were frightful. It was not just that the old, rickety tenements were packed with people, and were even more crowded in term-time when country families came to stay in the city so that their children could attend the schools there. It was also the mess in the streets, which some people said could be smelt six miles away in Dalkeith. Although every landlord had to provide rubbish bins which were emptied into carts each night, people living in the alleys off the main streets were still just chucking their refuse and the contents of their chamber-pots out into the street, often from a great height. There was a terrible amount of disease, too. One visitor wrote, 'When I was in bed I was forced to hide my head between the sheets; for the smell of the filth thrown out by the neighbours came pouring into the room to such a degree, I was almost poisoned with the stench.'

Something had to be done. In about 1770 work began on the building of a new town on the other side of the Nor' Loch, with a bridge joining it to the Old Town. Rules were laid down about the height of houses, their distance from the street and the materials of which they could be built. As a result, by 1820 the New Town of Edinburgh had become one of the grandest and most beautiful housing developments in the world.

The most usual kind of New Town house had a basement in which was the kitchen; a ground floor on which was the dining-room and, at the back, the main bedroom; and one or two storeys on top. The servants slept in small rooms in the basement or in the attic. A bell-board

in the kitchen worked by pulling wires summoned them to which-ever room in the house they were required. The main rooms of the house were large and airy, but very dark in winter. Edinburgh streets had gas lighting in 1817, but for many years after that, the houses continued to be lit by candles. Most houses were built with a water-pipe to the kitchen. Though a water-closet had now been invented, it simply flushed into a copper box underneath, which had to be taken away and emptied by a servant.

The 18th century was an age of magnificence in the building of country mansions too, often surrounded by elaborate gardens. Some were newly built. Others were made by enlarging existing castles, adding wings and towers at the sides, or putting new floors on top. There were drawing-rooms and dining-rooms (Blair Castle is said to have had three of each), countless bedrooms and dressing-rooms, rooms in which to play cards, a ballroom, galleries for displaying paintings and sculpture, a schoolroom and nurseries for the children. There was sometimes a chapel, too — the chapel at Glamis Castle had its own organ. Ceilings were of decorated plaster-work, from which hung glass chandeliers each holding masses of candles. The walls were papered or painted, and often set with huge mirrors which made the rooms look even larger and brighter. If to us there may seem a lot of spare space in the dining-rooms or drawing-rooms, it was not for lack of elegant and polished furniture, of oak, walnut or mahogany.

These houses need many servants. In 1740, the recently widowed Lady Grisell Baillie had 17 servants to look after her needs and those of her guests. She must have done a lot of entertaining. In one year, there were eaten in her house 166 joints of beef (the equivalent of five whole oxen), 12 lambs, 32 pigs, 344 lb of butter and several thousand eggs.

A cruck-framed country cottage with double walls of stones and between them a layer of sand, to give extra warmth. At one end is a hingin' lum, a chimney built into the gable-end of the house.

Robert Burns's father is said to have built with his own hands the cottage in which the poet was born. The walls were of clay, and the roof was made of turf supported on cupples. Inside there was just a living-room, a kitchen and the byre. In some parts of Scotland all the villagers joined in the work of building a clay house. Some mixed the clay with straw, others made it into bricks, and the more experienced ones did the actual building. In this way all the walls were finished in a few hours, after which everyone celebrated with a good dinner, plenty to drink, and music and dancing. It was a good way to round off a dirty and rather messy job. Presumably the owner of the house then put on the roof in his own time.

At last, a proper form of middle-sized country house was also being developed, which became the standard home of lairds, ministers, merchants, master-craftsmen and well-to-do farmers. The walls were of brick and smoothed stone, and the roof of tiles. It had two rooms on the ground floor (kitchen and living-room), and two or three bedrooms upstairs. However, extensions could easily be added to the ground floor at either end of the house, to make extra rooms.

The mechanical age was beginning, too. Cotton mills were being built by streams of fast-moving water which provided the power to drive the machines. The owners of some of these factories built blocks of one-roomed tenements to house their workers. The children worked too, long hours for no pay. In one such single room in Blantyre, David Livingstone, the future explorer, lived with his parents and four brothers and sisters. Workers who came to live in the new industrial village of New Lanark were luckier. The owner of the mill, Robert Owen, had strong ideas about cleanliness and education, and he also built for his workers a church, village store, school and dance hall.

Though the ordinary country people continued to live in much the same way as they had done for many years, some of them could now afford fine clothes, and most farm workers possessed a watch. However, their homes were tiny boxes of about 12 by 4 metres, of one or two rooms, with a few box-beds, a couple of cupboards, a chest of drawers, a table, a mirror and a few wooden chairs. Even so, in 1790, many farmer's houses of this kind contained also a grandfather-clock.

Livingstone's home

A dancing class at Robert Owen's school, where the children of his workers were taught from two until ten years' old. Then they went to work in his mill.

100 Years Ago

The great mansions of the early 19th century, like the New Town of Edinburgh, were built in imitation of the architecture of ancient Greece and Rome. After Queen Victoria came to the throne in 1837, many rich people preferred their homes to look more like those of the barons of medieval times. So Victorian mansions were rambling buildings with towers and battlements and cone-topped pinnacles. Even the smaller houses of the less well-to-do usually had at least one pinnacle.

No lady in Victorian times would dream of doing any housework herself. There were servants to cook and clean and dust and scrub and do the washing and look after the children and, most important, to fetch and carry things. Coal had to be carried up from the cellar and food from the kitchen. Water had to be heated and brought upstairs for the wash-basins and to fill the 'hip-baths' in which people took their bath. The dirty water then had to be emptied into jugs and carried all the way down again.

Food and rents were much cheaper than they are today, and wages were low. Shopkeepers and other people who owned small businesses were able to live comfortably in tenements of four or five rooms, and to have one or two servants.

Victorian houses were usually dark and were crammed with heavy, ornate furniture. Tables were draped with thick cloths with tasseled fringes. Every surface was covered with ornaments, china and framed photographs. More china and glass were displayed in glass-fronted cupboards.

In about 1880, Glasgow, because of its shipbuilding and engineering works, was one of the greatest industrial cities in Europe. Homes were needed for the thousands of workers who were flocking to the shipyards and factories. The homes in the old tenement blocks and the new ones which were hurriedly being built were not just small: they were also desperately overcrowded. In one tenement of two tiny rooms and a kitchen there were found to be sleeping 15 adults and two children — and one of the adults was a lodger!

However, most workers' tenements were even smaller. A 'room and kitchen' was just that: a room about 4 metres square with a bed-closet (a built-in bed with a door which could be closed), and a kitchen of about the same size. A 'single-end' was just the one room, which served as kitchen, living-room and bedroom for the whole family and any lodgers. Only towards the end of the 19th century was any attempt made to build a sink with running water into each tenement — before that people had to go down to a tap outside in the close. One lavatory served all the families living on that floor of the block.

Today

Modern homes have many things which help to make life easier and more comfortable. Ask your parents if, when they were children, their homes had a telephone, a television set, a washing machine, central heating. Then ask your grandparents about the homes in which they lived when they were children. Was there electric light? Hot water from a tap? A bath with running water? A refrigerator? Ask them all too what else there is in your home which they might not have had in theirs.

The outside appearance of the homes of many city people has changed, too. Complete new towns have been planned and built where there were no houses before, as at Cumbernauld, East Kilbride and Livingston. As well as homes, all the facilities which people need must be built too in the new towns — banks, shops, post offices, schools, libraries, swimming-pools.

In the cities themselves, vast areas of old slum houses have been flattened, both to replace them with better homes and to make way for new roads. One answer to providing better homes was to build high-rise blocks of flats. These tower up into the sky and can be seen from miles around, as indeed the people that planned them intended that they should. High-rise blocks take up less area of land than other kinds of housing. They can be set near parkland or right in the city itself.

Though in Glasgow and Edinburgh it had been a tradition for people to live in high buildings, the modern high-rise blocks have not been very popular. The new homes may have a kitchen and bath-room, electricity and central heating, and a front door which can be closed and locked. But many people did not want the privacy of their own self-contained flat. They missed the 'drying-green' on which everyone put out their washing to dry. They missed, too, the sharing and the friendliness, and chatting with neighbours out on the street pavements. They didn't like waiting for the lift, and having to walk up and down many stairs when it broke down. However, research has been done to improve the conditions of those living in high-rise flats, especially old people and those with children, and no more blocks of this kind are now being built.

What the site looked like in 1984.

A plan to restore part of the dockland of Leith to what it looked like more than 150 years ago, while providing new homes and offices on the water-side.

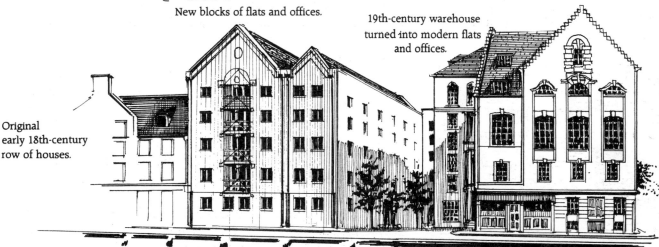

New blocks of flats and offices.

19th-century warehouse turned into modern flats and offices.

Original early 18th-century row of houses.

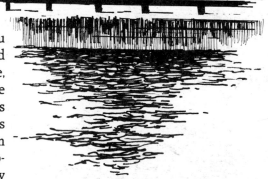

If you look at some of the newest houses and blocks of flats, you will see that the outsides of the buildings have often been designed to fit in with older buildings around them. In Culross, for instance, there is a modern block of flats which blends perfectly with the 16th-century houses nearby. Old churches and mills and breweries and warehouses are being turned into new blocks of flats, too. In this way, old buildings are preserved and the people who now live in them have homes with all the advantages which modern science can provide. Indeed, in some developments of this kind, the owner of a new flat can state exactly how he wants the rooms inside it to be laid out.

Places to Visit

Further details of these and other places to visit are in SCOTLAND — 1001 THINGS TO SEE, published by the Scottish Tourist Board.
Or ring or write to
Scottish Tourist Board,
PO Box 705,
Edinburgh EH4 3EU.
Tel: 031-332 2433.